Scenic Driving

MASSACHUSETTS

D1360400

Scenic Driving

MASSACHUSETTS

Exploring the State's Most Spectacular
Byways and Back Roads

STEWART M. GREEN

Globe
Pequot

Guilford, Connecticut

Globe Pequot

An imprint of Rowman & Littlefield

Distributed by NATIONAL BOOK NETWORK

Copyright © 2016 by Rowman and Littlefield

Photography by Stewart M. Green unless otherwise noted.

Excerpted from *Scenic Routes & Byways New England* (Globe Pequot, 978-0-7627-7955-0)

British Library Cataloguing in Publication Information Available

Library of Congress Cataloging-in-Publication Data Available

ISBN 978-1-4930-2239-7 (paperback)
ISBN 978-1-4930-2240-3 (e-book)

♾™ The paper used in this publication meets the minimum requirements of American National Standard for Information Sciences—Permanence of Paper for Printed Library Materials, ANSI/NISO Z39.48-1992.

TABLE OF CONTENTS

Massachusetts

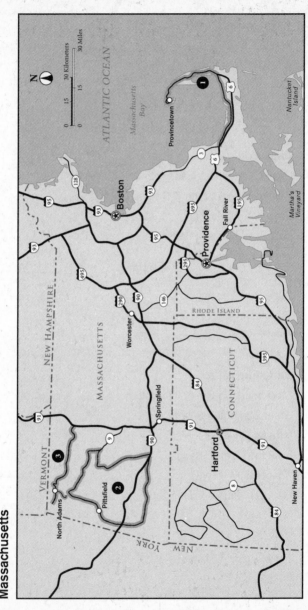

INTRODUCTION

Massachusetts offers travelers a spectacular assortment of natural and scenic wonders, historic sites, and varied recreational opportunities. Numerous state parks, forests, beaches, and recreation areas preserve slices of superlative landscapes. In addition to the ocean, thousands of lakes and ponds and numerous rivers and brooks offer boating, swimming, canoeing, and angling choices for outdoor enthusiasts. The cities, towns, and villages, from the urban centers to myriad tiny villages dotting the hills of Massachusetts, are filled with culture and steeped in history.

Scenic Driving Massachusetts is an indispensable mile-by-mile highway companion that explores and discovers the wonders of this compact region. The drives follow miles of highways and back roads, sampling the region's colorful history, beauty spots, hidden wonders, and scenic jewels. Drivers will wind along sandy beaches and headlands pounded by the restless ocean along the coast, marvel at classic villages set among valleys and hills, pass rural birthplaces and burial sites of the notable and the notorious, and wander among shifting sand dunes. Most of the drives leave the urban sprawl and interstate highways behind, setting off into the beautiful heart of the state.

Massachusetts is laced with highways and roads, some dating back to the earliest paths that once connected colonial settlements. Area natives will undoubtedly wonder why some roads are included and others omitted. These routes were chosen for their beauty, unique natural history, and historical implications. Omitted are worthy roads for one reason or another, but mostly due to the burgeoning development along those asphalt corridors in an amazing labyrinth of highway possibilities.

Use these described drives to win a new appreciation and understanding of this marvelous land. Take them as a starting point to embark on new adventures by seeking out other back-road gems.

Travel Advice

Be prepared for changing weather when traveling these scenic highways, especially in winter when snow and ice encase the roadways. All of the drives are paved two-lane highways that are regularly maintained. Services are available on all the drives, and every little village offers at least some basics during daylight hours. Use caution when driving. Many of the roads twist and wind through valleys and over mountains, with blind corners. Follow the posted speed limits and stay in your lane. Use occasional pullouts to allow faster traffic to safely pass. Watch for heavy traffic on some roads, particularly during summer vacation season and on fall-foliage weekends. Be extremely alert for animals crossing the asphalt. Take care at dusk, just after darkness falls, and in the early morning.

The region's fickle weather creates changeable and dangerous driving conditions. Make sure your windshield wipers are in good shape. Heavy rain can impair highway vision and cause your vehicle to hydroplane. Snow and ice slicken mountain highways. Slow down, carry chains and a shovel, and have spare clothes and a sleeping bag when traveling in winter. Watch for fog and poor visibility, particularly along the coastlines. Know your vehicle and its limits when traveling and, above all, use common sense.

Travelers are, unfortunately, potential crime victims. Use caution when driving in urban areas or popular tourist destinations. Keep all valuables, including wallets, purses, cameras, and video cameras, out of sight in a parked car. Better yet, take them with you when leaving the vehicle.

These drives cross a complex mosaic of private and public land. Respect private property rights by not trespassing or crossing fences.

Remember also that all archaeological and historic sites are protected by federal law. Campers should try to use established campgrounds or campsites whenever possible to avoid adverse environmental impacts. Remember to douse your campfires and to pack all your trash out with you to the nearest refuse container.

Every road we travel offers its own promise and special rewards. Remember Walt Whitman's poetic proclamation as you drive along these scenic highways: "Afoot, light-hearted, I take to the open road. Healthy, free, the world before me."

Legend

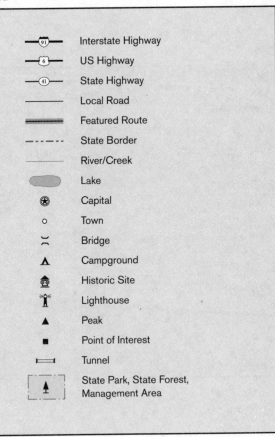

—(91)—	Interstate Highway
—(6)—	US Highway
—(41)—	State Highway
———	Local Road
▬▬▬	Featured Route
- - - - -	State Border
———	River/Creek
⬭	Lake
⊛	Capital
○	Town
⌣	Bridge
▲	Campground
🏛	Historic Site
🗼	Lighthouse
▲	Peak
■	Point of Interest
⊢⊣	Tunnel
⌐▲¬	State Park, State Forest, Management Area

Cape Cod

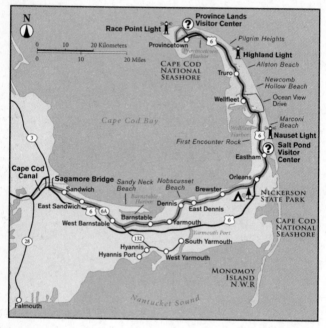

1 Cape Cod

General description: A 63-mile scenic route along the historic south shore of Cape Cod Bay and up the Outer Beach along the Atlantic Ocean in Cape Cod National Seashore to Provincetown at the Cape's northern tip.

Special attractions: Heritage Plantation, Sandwich Historical Museum, Crocker Tavern, Cape Cod Museum of Natural History, Nickerson State Park, Cape Cod National Seashore, Nauset Beach and Light, Marconi Beach and Station Site, Race Point, Salt Pond Visitor Center, Province Lands Visitor Center, Old Harbor Life Saving Station, Three Sisters Lighthouse, trails, hiking, picnicking, beaches, biking, birding, fishing, children's programs.

Location: Southeastern Massachusetts.

Drive route numbers: MA 6A, US 6.

Travel season: Year-round.

Camping: Nickerson State Park offers 420 campsites. Shawme-Crowell State Forest, near the Cape Cod Canal, has a 285-site campground. Visit reserveamerica.com for reservations at any Massachusetts state forest and park campground. Otherwise, several private campgrounds are available on Cape Cod.

Services: All services in Sandwich, West Barnstable, Barnstable, Yarmouth, Dennis, Brewster, Orleans, Eastham, South Wellfleet, Wellfleet, Truro, and Provincetown.

Nearby attractions: Woods Hole, Martha's Vineyard, Nantucket Island, Monomoy National Wildlife Refuge, Aptucxet Trading Post, Myles Standish State Forest, Plymouth Rock, Plymouth Plantation, Boston attractions.

The Route

Like a flexed, muscular, 60-mile-long arm, Cape Cod bends far out into the Atlantic Ocean from the southeastern corner of Massachusetts. This long, crooked peninsula, bordered by 585 miles of shoreline and 310 miles of sand beaches, is a quintessential New England landscape. When anyone talks of the great natural wonders of the Northeast, the Cape is always the first one mentioned—and for good reason. Here lies a magnificent landscape shaped by the Earth's most basic elements: storm and sunlight; the unceasing wind constantly resculpting sand dunes; and the restless North Atlantic pounding against the outer edges.

This 63-mile drive, beginning at the Cape Cod Canal and ending at the tip of the Cape, follows a spectacular transition zone between land and sea, skirting salt marshes and cranberry bogs; passing quiet estuaries, ponds, inlets, and coves; running along one of New England's longest sand beaches; threading through miniature forests of pitch pine and scrub oak; and crossing sand dunes anchored by beach grass. Be warned, however, that much of the Cape has succumbed to tacky strip malls, fast-food joints, factory outlet stores, and other businesses out to separate travelers from their money. Fortunately it's easy to look beyond the T-shirt shops and see the enduring beauty of this outermost land.

The Cape offers a year-round travel climate, with each season lending a distinct flavor to the journey. Summers are the traditional beach season, with vacationers flocking onto the beaches and filling the campgrounds and trails. Weather is generally mild in summer with daily highs rising into the 80s, sunny skies, and warm water. The ocean is generally warmest in August and September. Autumns are superb. Daytime temperatures range from 50 to 70 degrees with brisk nights, little precipitation, and fewer folks to share the beach. Winter, with its heavy seas, cold temperatures, and windy conditions, might not seem like an ideal time to travel Cape Cod, but stalwart visitors will have the place to themselves. Snowfall is usually moderate. Spring is a short, fickle season. Expect cool to warm temperatures, occasional foggy or rainy days, and wind.

The drive follows MA 6A to US 6 at Orleans. This route, called the King's Highway, is one of the oldest roads in the United

States. US 6 offers a quick return trip from Orleans to Sagamore and the mainland on a limited-access, four-lane highway. The highways usually offer easy driving with localized congestion. Be advised, however, that weekends and holidays, particularly in summer, are entirely different. Cape Cod's highways are often clogged with legendary stop-and-go traffic jams in morning and evening. Only two bridges cross the Cape Cod Canal, choking the arteries leading to them. It's best to time your trip for quieter times of the week.

Cape Cod Canal & Sandwich

The drive begins at the Sagamore Bridge over the **Cape Cod Canal,** a 17.4-mile-long, 500-foot-wide ditch (the widest sea level canal in the world) that severs the Cape's arm from the mainland at its narrow shoulder joint. The canal, used by more than 20,000 vessels annually, effectively makes the peninsula into an island. The idea for a trans-Cape canal originated back in 1624, when Pilgrim Myles Standish realized a canal would increase trade between the Plymouth Colony and the Dutch at New Amsterdam. George Washington later ordered a survey and saw plans drawn up for the canal, but the project was shelved. The first canal, financed by millionaire August Belmont, opened in 1914 after almost 40 years of work. The narrow, one-way canal, slicing off more than 100 miles from the Boston to New York connections, didn't begin generating revenue and traffic until the US Army Corps of Engineers widened and deepened it. The two graceful steel spans, the Sagamore and Bourne bridges, were completed in 1935.

Begin the drive by crossing the arched **Sagamore Bridge** on US 6 then exiting immediately at exit 1 onto MA 6A, the old King's Highway. The road swings east along the canal, passing under the bridge, and heads onto the Upper Cape, the section nearest the mainland. The Mid Cape is exactly what it sounds like—the midsection between the biceps and elbow of the flexed "arm." The Lower Cape is the outer forearm section, which extends northward.

Just past the bridge the drive enters the quaint 1637 town of **Sandwich,** the oldest settlement on Cape Cod. The area was originally settled in 1627 when Pilgrims built the Aptucxet Trading Post as a commerce center for Indians and Dutch and English colonists west of today's town. Ten years later, Edmund Freeman and some followers moved here from Saugus on the coast north of Boston. By 1669 the town had grown enough to become incorporated and was named after a village in Kent, England, where many of the pioneer families had originated. Quakers later settled in Sandwich, but were persecuted by the Puritan majority. Eventually they were tolerated, and the town now boasts the oldest continuous Quaker meeting in America, begun in 1657.

The lack of a harbor kept Sandwich from growing as a maritime center, so the town relied instead on whaling and local farming for sustenance. In the early 19th century, Sandwich began a glass-making tradition, using the abundant local sand or silica and sodium chloride, which is now preserved in the Sandwich Glass Museum. The Boston & Sandwich Glass Company created a wide range of glass objects that today are coveted by collectors. The factory, founded in 1825, was shut down during an 1888 labor dispute and never reopened.

Sandwich now retains much of its old charm and history in the **Town Hall Square Historic District,** a collection of 47 houses, some dating from the 1600s, and the elegant 1834 Town Hall. The village offers a potpourri of classic New England architecture, including saltboxes from the 1700s, Federal and Gothic Revival–style houses and buildings, and the famed and often imitated Cape Cod cottages. The town's 1847 First Church of Christ now houses one of New England's oldest congregations, initially gathered in 1637 by the first Pilgrim settlers.

A host of interesting museums and domiciles are found in the immediate environs of Sandwich. Some of the best surround

Shawme Lake, a pond created by early residents to generate power for milling. The **Hoxie House,** built in 1637, has thick timbers and recessed windows, and is reputed to be the oldest house still standing on the Cape and, outside the Pueblo and Hopi villages in the Southwest, among the oldest dwellings in the United States. This classic saltbox, once the home of whaling captain Abraham Hoxie, has been restored and furnished to the 1680 era. It is open for tours in summer.

Nearby is **Thomas Dexter's Grist Mill,** used from the 1650s until the late 1800s and now restored to grind grain the old-fashioned way. The **Thornton Burgess Museum** honors a local naturalist and children's author with a collection of his memorabilia and natural history exhibits. Also near the pond is the old Sandwich burying ground, with some slate gravestones from the 1680s. A headstone of interest sits atop the 1677 grave of Sandwich founder Edmund Freeman in a grove of pines on Wilson Road. Freeman is buried under a saddle next to his wife, Elizabeth, who lies under a pillion, a chair attached to a saddle so two people can ride side by side. In this case, that ride went into eternity.

The last attraction of note at Sandwich is the **Heritage Plantation,** off MA 130. This fascinating place, covering 76 landscaped acres, includes gardens, woods, ponds, and several diverse museums. The area was once the private estate of industrialist Charles Breeder, who indulged in creating hybrid rhododendrons during his 22-year retirement. The blossoms in May and June are simply stunning, and worth a visit for that alone. The plantation offers a slew of other sights, however. A replica of the round Hancock Shaker Barn from the Berkshires houses a collection of 34 antique and classic autos, including Gary Cooper's 1931 custom yellow Duesenberg and President Taft's 1909 White Steamer, the first official presidential limo. A Military Museum houses antique weapons, more than 2,000 miniature figures, and flags that have flown over the United States. Other collections include artworks, Currier & Ives lithographs, American folk art, and Indian artifacts.

Just north of town is the Sandwich town beach, a lovely and quiet beach reached by a boardwalk across a salt marsh. On the southwest shore of Cape Cod Bay, both the beach and the marsh are popular birding areas.

Barnstable, Yarmouth & Dennis

The drive heads southeast from Sandwich, rolling through low, undulating hills dotted with houses. Two large salt marshes, fed by seawater that floods Scorton Creek, flank the asphalt. Down the road lie the towns of West Barnstable and, in just a few miles, **Barnstable. West Barnstable** is a small village with an assortment of shops and restaurants. The village's 1717 West Parish Congregational Church is considered the denomination's oldest church building. Its half-ton bell was cast by patriot Paul Revere. Sandy Neck Road, just west of the town, leads northeast to the excellent barrier beach of Sandy Neck. The 8-mile neck, built of beach sand and dunes, separates Cape Cod Bay from Barnstable Harbor. The small parking lot charges a fee and fills quickly on weekends, since it offers easy access to this quiet beach.

Barnstable, encompassing the communities of Barnstable, Hyannis, Cotuit, Santuit, Osterville, Centerville, and Cummaquid, is the Cape's largest town. This was the Cape's second village, established in 1639 by a separatist Puritan parish that had originally landed at Scituate in 1634. By the 1700s the town and its protected harbor flourished as a rum trading and whaling port. The Sturgis Library, named for local trading tycoon William Sturgis, is the oldest public library building in the United States. Part of the library is a 1644 house. In addition to such rich history, the Barnstable area also offers bed-and-breakfasts, restaurants, and shops.

Three miles past Barnstable MA 6A runs through **Yarmouth,** the third village established on the Cape. Settled in 1639, Yarmouth and its neighbor **Yarmouth Port** thrived in the mid-19th century as seafaring towns. The 1740 Captain Bangs Hallet House, run by the local historical society, preserves a slice of this heritage. Several botanical trails begin at the house and thread across 53 nearby acres. Other preserved Yarmouth houses are the **Taylor-Bray Farm,** an old shipyard and farm, and the **Winslow-Crocker House,** which was built in 1780 in Barnstable but taken down and reassembled at Yarmouth in 1935. **Hallet's Store,** a turn-of-the-last-century drugstore and soda fountain in Yarmouth Port, is a nostalgic stop. **Grey's Beach,** a municipal beach on the warm-water bay, is about the only town beach here that doesn't charge a daily fee.

The drive continues to **Dennis,** the next classic old Cape village, and East Dennis. The town was originally part of Yarmouth but separated in 1793, taking the name of Reverend Josiah Dennis, the popular pastor of its first meetinghouse. Like Yarmouth, Dennis was a seagoing village. The Shiverick Shipyards at Sesuit Harbor built many clipper ships, schooners, and packet boats in the early 1800s. In 1837 the town boasted more than 150 captains basing vessels out of Dennis. The **Josiah Dennis Manse,** the 1736 home of the village's namesake, offers free tours of the restored, furnished house. Other points of interest are the Cape Museum of Fine Arts, the Cape Playhouse, and the 1801 Jericho House and Barn Museum. The 30-foot-high **Scargo Tower,** just off the highway, is a stone tower that yields superb views of Cape Cod Bay, the long sandy Cape peninsula, and Provincetown with its tall Pilgrim Monument on a clear day. Just east of town near Scargo Lake and the tower is the Nobscusset Indian burial ground.

Brewster & Orleans

The drive leaves East Dennis and enters **Brewster,** the last of the historic towns on the Mid Cape. Brewster, settled in 1656 and named for William Brewster from the Plymouth Colony across the bay, is a lovely, rural town spread along elm-lined MA 6A. Despite its lack of a port, Brewster was a thriving sea

A salt marsh in Brewster, MA THINKSTOCK

captains' village. One of its more famed seamen was Captain Dave Nickerson, whose adopted son René Rousseau was, legend has it, the Dauphin. The child, supposedly the son of French King Louis XVI and Marie Antoinette, was given to Nickerson by a veiled woman in the war-torn streets of revolutionary Paris in 1789 to save him from certain death. Brewster's captains also defied the American trade embargo with the British in the unpopular War of 1812 by continuing their shipping business. After the war the sailors brought vast wealth from around the world to their Brewster home base, making immense fortunes and building huge houses. The private Dillingham House, built about 1660 by Captain John Dillingham, is possibly the Cape's second-oldest existing house.

A host of visitor attractions scatter across Brewster. One of the best is the restored 1873 **Stony Brook Grist Mill and Museum.** The picturesque, water-powered mill, set along Stony Brook Pond, offers milling demonstrations through summer. An annual spawning run of herring, or alewives, going from Cape Cod Bay to inland freshwater ponds passes the mill via a fish ladder in late spring. Other attractions include the Cape Cod Museum of Natural History, with displays on the Cape's ecology and history, a weather station, and three trails; **Drummer Boy Museum,** illustrating scenes from the Revolution; and the fascinating **New England Fire and History Museum.** This last museum exhibits a great collection of fire equipment, including hand- and horse-drawn fire engines, old fire helmets, a diorama detailing Chicago's 1871 fire, and an old firehouse.

Nickerson State Park sprawls along the eastern edge of Brewster. The inland park, covering 1,955 acres, is a pitch pine and oak woodland dotted with 8 ponds and threaded with trails. The ponds are glacial features called kettle ponds that formed when large chunks of a melting glacier dropped into the ground

The Brewster Store, originally an 1852 church, was opened as a general store in 1866 by William Knowles.

and were blanketed with other debris. Later the ice melted, leaving these small ponds in the resulting depressions. The park's bayside section, north of MA 6A, has a large salt marsh, coastal dunes, and tidal flats. The park offers a wide assortment of outdoor recreation, including boating on Cliff Pond, picnicking, hiking, biking on the **Cape Cod Rail Trail,** trout fishing in the stocked ponds, and camping in the 420-site campground. This campground also makes a great base camp for exploring the upper parts of Cape Cod.

From Nickerson State Park the drive continues east and in 1.5 miles reaches US 6 and the town of **Orleans.** Turn left (north) onto US 6, which runs through piney sand hills west of Orleans and a couple of miles later reaches a rotary. Continue north on US 6.

Orleans, bypassed by the route, is the busy gateway to **Cape Cod National Seashore.** Lying on the southwest shore of Town Cove, the town was settled in 1693 and called Nauset, but was later renamed for the exiled Duke of Orleans, Louis Philippe de Bourbon, who visited here in 1797. As the commercial hub for the Lower Cape, Orleans offers numerous accommodation choices, restaurants, and shops. A few points of interest here include the **Orleans Historical Society**'s collection in the 1834 Greek Revival–style Meeting House, and the **French Cable Museum** with cables and transmission equipment from the 1879 trans-Atlantic telegraph system between Orleans and Brest, France. Orleans has a dual coastline, with its Rock Harbor and Skaket Beach opening onto placid Cape Cod Bay to the west. Nauset Beach, accessed from Beach Road, is a gorgeous swath of sandy beach that stretches south from here to Chatham.

The highway bends northeast after bypassing Orleans, running along Town Cove. The right turn to the **Fort Hill** area in Cape Cod National Seashore is 1.5 miles from the rotary. The

Cape Cod offers miles of sandy beaches, such as Nauset Light Beach, that front the Atlantic Ocean.

The picturesque Nauset Beach Light, perched on a bluff, has warned sailors of offshore dangers since 1877.

road runs back to parking lots on a low rise above **Nauset Marsh.** The 1.5-mile **Fort Hill Trail** begins across from the Penniman House, dropping across fields with old stone walls and house sites to some good views of Nauset Marsh before following the Red Maple Swamp Trail back to the parking area. The landmark Empire-style **Penniman House** was built in 1868 by whaling captain Edward Penniman. The fort at the end of the road was the apparent site of an earthen breastworks fort erected in 1653 during a Dutch–English conflict. Later the area was cleared and tilled as part of Reverend Samuel Treat's farm.

Cape Cod National Seashore

Back on the drive, the highway runs north to the national seashore's **Salt Pond Visitor Center** in Eastham. The center, open daily, is a great place to pick up maps, visitor information, and a schedule of Salt Pond interpretative programs. Displays on the Cape's natural history, geology, and history as well as an introductory video educate visitors to this seaside world. The Nauset Marsh Trail also begins at the center. Since 1961 most of Cape Cod north from here to the tip has been protected in 43,608-acre Cape Cod National Seashore, the nation's first designated seashore administered by the National Park Service. This 40-mile stretch of land, fronted by the chilly North Atlantic Ocean, is a much different and wilder landscape than that traversed by the first section of this drive along the south shore of Cape Cod Bay. This is a place of open beaches, flanked by sand dunes and marshes, and fewer villages. The parkland offers a wealth of natural areas, historic sites, and things to do.

Cape Cod boasts a long and colorful history that began as the 3,500-year-old homeland of the Wampanoag Indians, although earlier archaeological sites date to nearly 9,000 years ago. The Algonquin-speaking Wampanoags, living in villages on the Cape, survived by fishing and farming. Explorer Samuel de Champlain noted in 1605 that the Indians grew corn, squash, beans, and tobacco, and stored corn in buried grass sacks. European exploration of Cape Cod possibly began in AD 1003 when mariner Leif Ericson and his Viking crew landed on Nauset, calling it "Wonderstrand." The Cape was the first landfall for later explorers, including Englishman Bartholomew Gosnold, who named it Cape Cod in 1602 for "the great store of cod fish."

This cape was also the first landing site of the Pilgrims in early November 1620 after a 65-day journey from Holland. Although they intended to sail south to the Hudson River, they decided to look at this area for possible settlement. The *Mayflower* anchored off today's Provincetown; the Pilgrims drew up and signed the Mayflower Compact to govern themselves, then set about exploring the Cape and the bay. Near Eastham a party led by Myles Standish was attacked by Indian arrows at First Encounter Beach. Musket fire was returned, and both sides retreated with no injuries. A plaque marks the spot today. By mid-December the Pilgrims finally decided to settle across the bay at

Plymouth, finding Cape Cod, in one Pilgrim's words, "a hidious and desolate wildernes."

Eastham to Wellfleet

Eastham, one of the original towns on Cape Cod, was settled in 1644 by 49 Pilgrims from the Plymouth Colony. The village grew as an agricultural center, despite the damage that blackbirds and crows did to crops. A 1667 law forced every household to kill twelve blackbirds or three crows a year. The stakes were upped in 1695 when another ordinance forbid any bachelor from marrying unless his annual bird quota was fulfilled. Later Eastham become a fishing, whaling, and trading port. The town's past is displayed by the local historical society in the 1869 **Eastham Schoolhouse Museum.** The building, across from the Salt Pond Visitor Center, has an entrance framed by the jawbones of a great whale. Just south on US 6 is the 1680 **Eastham Windmill,** the oldest windmill on Cape Cod. It was built in 1680 in Plymouth and subsequently moved to Truro and then Eastham in 1793. The octagonal tower was used to grind grain for flour. The town's Old Cove Cemetery is the burial ground of many early Eastham settlers, including three of the Mayflower Pilgrims, who died in 1620.

US 6 heads north from Eastham along haphazard strip development to **Wellfleet.** Both Doane and Nauset Cable Roads lead east to Coast Guard Beach and Nauset Light Beach along the shore. **Nauset Beach Light,** possibly the Cape's most spectacular lighthouse, perches on a bluff above the beach. Three stone towers topped with lights, called the Three Sisters by sailors, were first built here in 1838 but collapsed as sand was eroded from their base. The lighthouse warns mariners of the many offshore dangers that lurk along Cape Cod's Atlantic coast. Dense fog, fierce storms, and hurricanes have conspired with hidden sandbars, shoals, and rip tides to sink more than 3,000 ships in these treacherous waters since the Sparrowhawk, an English ship, ran aground off Orleans in 1626. The worst wreck occurred in 1898 when 175 people went down off Truro on the steamship Portland in a terrible gale. After the Cape Cod Canal opened in 1914, shipping losses went down dramatically. Radar, sonar, and other navigational equipment have further reduced underwater dangers. The historic lighthouse was moved 300 feet west of an eroding cliff in 1996.

Continuing the drive, the highway passes the 1,100-acre Audubon Society's **Wellfleet Bay Wildlife Sanctuary** along a cove on the bay side. A right turn leads to Marconi Beach and Marconi Station Site. **Marconi Station** is the site of the first wireless trans-Atlantic radio broadcast. When Italian engineer Guglielmo Marconi experimented with radio communication, he selected this remote high point above the beach to build four 210-foot towers and a transmitting station. On January 18, 1903, he succeeded in sending a Morse code message from President Theodore Roosevelt to England's King Edward VII. Soon afterwards the wireless became the chosen mode of communication, especially between ships. The Marconi Station picked up the 1912 distress call from the luxury liner *Titanic* after it struck an iceberg. The station was closed in 1917 and dismantled 4 years later. Little remains at the site today, except two of the four tower foundations. Marconi's towers, now on the edge of cliffs, were originally set back 165 feet from the sandy edge. The restless surf has eroded the bluffs in the intervening years so that this historical site sits on the edge of the sea.

The **Atlantic White Cedar Swamp Trail** begins on the opposite side of the Marconi Station parking area. This 1-mile footpath is an excellent hike through some diverse woodlands. The trail initially passes through a pygmy forest of bear or scrub oak, beach heather, crowberry, and stunted pitch pines. The trees, including white and black oaks, become taller farther inland. Finally a boardwalk loops through a swampy peatland in a kettle pond left by a retreating glacier. Here grows a magnificent stand of Atlantic white cedar, a light, rot-resistant wood that was prized for lumber in colonial New England.

The 48-foot Nauset Beach Light is preserved at Cape Cod National Seashore. THINKSTOCK

The drive continues north to **Wellfleet,** a splendid town centered around its harbor on Wellfleet Bay. Incorporated in 1763, the town was named for the Wellfleet oyster beds in England. It prospered early from its own oyster beds and as a fishing port. In 1606 passing explorer Samuel de Champlain dubbed it Oyster Port. Even today Wellfleet is a working fishing town, with its shellfish industry generating more than $10 million annually. Wellfleet is also the hometown of the United Fruit Company, an enterprise started by sea captain Lorenzo Dow Baker in the 1870s as a banana importer. The Wellfleet Historical Society Museum displays items from the area's past, including farm tools, weapons, and everyday household items. The town also offers numerous shops and art galleries along with the usual assortment of dining establishments and hotels.

A good side-trip leads west from town on Chequesset Neck Road to **Great Island,** part of the national seashore. A trail begins from a picnic area and heads south onto Great Island, a thin peninsula that stretches its sandy spit south into Cape Cod Bay. East of Wellfleet is Ocean View Drive. Reach it by turning east on Le Count Hollow Road. The drive runs along the dramatic coastline atop sand cliffs. A number of town-managed beaches lie below the asphalt. Beyond the road spreads the great expanse of ocean, with its frothy surf pounding against the shore.

Truro

Farther north on the drive is **Truro.** This village, probably the least commercialized of the towns on the Lower Cape, sits amid sand dunes on the Pamet River. The Truro area boasts an early Pilgrim association. Myles Standish discovered a buried cache of Indian corn on what is now known as **Corn Hill.** The hungry men took the corn, and Standish eventually paid its rightful owner the following year for its use. The town was first settled by a group of Pilgrims called the Pamet Proprietors in 1689, and took the name Truro at its incorporation in 1709 because of its similarities to a Cornish seaside area in England. Truro, like Wellfleet, was a longtime fishing village that harvested cod and whales. A ferocious storm in October 1841 decimated its population by killing 57 town fishermen. Most were caught while fishing on Georges Banks or making the desperate journey home. The next day more than 100 bodies were recovered along the Cape's sandy shores.

The Truro area offers many points of interest. Two good hikes are the 0.5-mile **Pamet Cranberry Bog Trail**, exploring an abandoned cranberry operation, and the 0.75-mile **Pilgrim Spring Trail,** which leads to the spring where the Pilgrims drank their first fresh water in New England. The 66-foot-tall **Highland Light or Cape Cod Light** is the oldest lighthouse on Cape Cod. The first light was erected in 1798 to steer ships away from this treacherous stretch of beach. Today's automated lighthouse, perched atop 120-foot cliffs of sand, gravel, stones, and boulders, was built in 1857. The Coast Guard maintains a radio beacon here to orient passing ships. Nearby is the Highland Golf Course, built in 1892, and the **Highland House Museum,** housed in an old inn, with a collection of artifacts from shipwrecks, whaling relics, old guns, and Sandwich glass.

Cape Cod Geology

As the drive heads north from the developed part of Truro, the Cape narrows and appears more desolate than the wooded southern parts. Out here this becomes a place defined first and foremost by the ocean. The Cape, the easternmost point of American land in the Atlantic Ocean, is rocked by the full fury of the famed nor'easter storms. In late fall the prevailing winds gradually shift to the north and east, and the resulting violent winter gales begin to erode away the cliffs, beaches, and barrier dunes. The average rate of cliff erosion on the outer Cape escarpment above the beaches is between 2 and 4 feet a year. Since the Pilgrims landed almost 400 years ago, the alterations to the

The Highland Light at North Truro is the oldest and tallest lighthouse on Cape Cod. THINKSTOCK

shoreline have been momentous and closely linked to the Cape's tenuous relationship with water, tides, wind, and weather.

Cape Cod is, in a sense, a momentary landscape, a transitory hook on the edge of North America. The world's largest glacial peninsula, the Cape is one of our newest landforms and will likely be one of the first erased from the continent. It was deposited a scant 25,000 years ago by an immense, retreating ice sheet that reached a thickness of some 10,000 feet. During that glacial period much of the world's water was encased in ice and the ocean level was about 400 feet lower than today. As the climate warmed, the glacier began melting and retreating northward. The ice sheet departed 17,000 years ago, leaving huge moraines—vast deposits of broken rock debris and glacial till or a rough assortment of sand, pebbles, cobbles, and boulders—and outwash plains on a now-submerged coastal surface that became Cape Cod, Martha's Vineyard, and Nantucket Island.

The drive continues north, following the northwest bend of the Cape's bent wrist. At **Pilgrim Heights** are the **Pilgrim Spring** and **Small Swamp trails,** along with a picnic area. Past that is brackish **Pilgrim Lake,** a large body of water edged by the highway on the south and a sizable region of parabolic sand dunes on the northeast. The lake is separated from the harbor by a long dike constructed in 1869 to protect the harbor and its fishing industry from the ocean. The highway runs into Provincetown, a picturesque town rimming Provincetown Harbor, one of the Cape's best anchorages.

Provincetown

Provincetown, or "P-town" to locals, is a busy, crowded town with narrow streets crammed with shops, restaurants, and hotels. The town, the first landing place of the Pilgrims, has been a whaling

An eclectic mixture of tourists and locals crowd Commercial Street in the heart of Provincetown.

and fishing port, trading hub, and artists' colony. On November 11, 1620, the Mayflower, navigating through sandy shoals around Race Point, anchored in "ye Capeharbor wher they ridd in saftie." A party of Pilgrims came ashore here that day and "fell upon their knees and blessed ye God of heaven, who had brought them over ye vast and furious ocean" five weeks before they decided to settle across the bay in Plymouth. P-town locals and Cape Codders always want to set the record straight—the Pilgrims came here first, and Plymouth was merely an afterthought. The 250-foot-high granite Pilgrim Monument, built in 1907 and supposedly the tallest granite building in the world, commemorates the Pilgrims' landing here and their subsequent colonization of Massachusetts. The top of the tower, 352 feet above sea level, affords a marvelous view of the ocean, the bay, the sandy Province Lands at Race Point, and, on a clear day, a glimpse of the mainland.

The town, with its protected harbor, is a superb fishing port. It flourished through the 19th century with great catches of cod from the fertile offshore banks. Many Portuguese fishermen migrated here from the Azores Islands and the Lisbon area for the good fishing a century ago. Their descendants make up much of the town's permanent population. The town has also been a famed artists' colony, beginning with the founding of the Cape Cod School of Art in 1901 by portrait painter Charles Hawthorne. Painters, writers, and playwrights have flocked here ever since to experience the airy, translucent light of this village by the sea.

Colorful Provincetown is Cape Cod's most popular and fascinating town, and is usually bustling—particularly in summer, when it fills to capacity with a weekend population of 100,000. Reservations for overnight stays are a must. Commercial Street, the main thoroughfare, jams with tourists and locals. Many boutiques and shops offer hours of browsing. An eclectic selection of eateries including chowder bars, seafood, and Portuguese cuisine keep the hungry amused. Art galleries, the largest concentration on the Cape, line the streets. Points of interest include the **Provincetown Heritage Museum** and **MacMillan**

Wharf, where the town fishing fleet anchors and whale-watching cruises originate.

The Province Lands

The last part of this drive enters Provincetown on US 6 and turns right (north) onto Race Point Road. This road winds through grass-covered dunes and beech and oak forests to **Race Point** and the northern edge of Cape Cod. **Province Lands Visitor Center,** offering information and maps, has a great observation deck with sweeping panoramic views of Provincetown, the dunes, and the ocean. The center has exhibits on the Cape's natural and human history, and naturalist-led walks and talks. Several trails for hikers and bicyclists begin here and wander out into the dune field, passing through stunted woods and exploring the Province Lands. At **Race Point Beach** is the **Old Harbor Life Saving Museum** housed in a life-saving station transported here from Chatham in 1977. The museum displays artifacts and relics from the 19th US Life Saving Service.

The Province Lands, the Cape region lying north of Provincetown, make up the newest part of Cape Cod. The area is a post-glacial deposit about 5,000 years old, formed of sand and alluvial material shifted from the Atlantic side of the Cape to the long sand spit southwest of Provincetown. Most of this young area is composed of sand dunes that are swept by wind and held mostly in place by beach grass, heather, and occasional woodlands. When the Pilgrims landed here, trees and shrubs anchored the sand. After settlement, however, the dunes were laid bare when the forest was cut for building and firewood, and cattle were let loose to graze the fragile ecosystem.

The great beach at Race Point is a fitting climax to Cape Cod. This long beach, edged by sand dunes and rimmed by the cold expanse of the North Atlantic, feels like the watery edge of the continent. Stand here in the wind and sun, where the relentless surf washes against your feet. A seagull wheels against the azure sky. A fishing boat slowly disappears beyond the ocean horizon. This is an elemental place, far removed from the clamor of nearby Provincetown. All that matters here is the lonely sea and sky.

Return to Provincetown from Race Point via the Province Lands Road, which runs down onto the west side of the tip, passes Herring Cove Beach, and bends inland back to Provincetown. Retrace US 6 back to the Cape Cod Canal to complete the journey.

2 Berkshire Hills

General description: A 132-mile loop drive through the scenic Berkshire Hills in western Massachusetts.

Special attractions: Hancock Shaker Village, Great Barrington State Forest, Albert Schweitzer Center, Monument Mountain Reservation, East Mountain State Forest, Bidwell House, Otis Ridge Ski Area, Beartown State Forest, Mount Greylock State Reservation, Berkshire Museum, Arrowhead, Pittsfield State Forest, Chesterfield Gorge, camping, hiking, historic sites, scenic views, fishing.

Location: Western Massachusetts. The drive begins and ends at exit 1 on the Massachusetts Turnpike.

Drive route numbers: US 20, MA 41, 23, 112, 116, 8, and 41.

Travel season: Year-round. Snow and ice can close or slicken roads in winter.

Camping: Beartown Mountain State Forest east of Great Barrington off MA 23 has a 12-site campground. Tolland State Forest, south of MA 23 near Otis, has a 93-site campground alongside Otis Reservoir. Chester Blandford State Forest, north of Blandford, has a 15-site campground. DAR State Forest north of Goshen, off MA 112, has a 51-site campground. Windsor State Forest, off MA 9 south of MA 116, has a 24-site campground. Mount Greylock State Reservation, west of Adams, has a 35-site campground. Pittsfield State Forest, northwest of Pittsfield and US 20, offers 25 campsites in 2 areas. October Mountain State Forest, southeast of Pittsfield, has a 47-site campground. Mount Washington State Forest, southwest of Great Barrington, has 15 primitive sites.

Services: All services in Adams, Pittsfield, and Great Barrington. Limited or seasonal services in the small towns along the drive.

Nearby attractions: Bartholomew's Cobble, Colonel Ashley House, Bish Bash State Forest, Berkshire Opera, Tanglewood, Lenox, Stockbridge, Chesterwood Museum, Norman Rockwell Museum, Berkshire Theater Festival, Williamstown, Clark Art Institute,

Berkshire Hills

Williams College Museum of Art, Taconic Trail State Park, Western Gateway Heritage State Park, Natural Bridge State Park, William Cullen Bryant Homestead, Bennington (VT), Litchfield Hills (CT).

The Route

The 132-mile Berkshire Hills Scenic Route makes a wide loop across the wooded hills and valleys of western Massachusetts, avoiding all the main thoroughfares such as US 7 and the tourist towns. Instead, the drive follows rural highways and quiet back roads through some of the region's loveliest countryside.

Every New England landscape is found here—thick woodlands punctuated by serene ponds and lakes; ancient, worn hills gentled by time and erosion; bucolic villages topped by slender church spires; open pastures and farms interrupted by stone fences, silver silos, orchards, and grazing Holsteins; rivers that wander between grass-lined banks; and tumbling brooks that shatter to foam over cliffs. The drive, with its many natural wonders (including Mount Greylock) and marvelous historic sites (including Hancock Shaker Village), easily takes a full day to enjoy.

The **Berkshire Hills** cover the western third of the Bay State, forming a high barrier that long impeded westward travel and settlement. The hills are the southern extension of Vermont's Green Mountains, the eroded roots of an ancient mountain range that rose over New England some 440 million years ago. Erosion slowly leveled the once lofty peaks down to an almost flat plain studded with occasional mountains, including Maine's Mount Katahdin, New Hampshire's Mount Monadnock, and Massachusetts's Mount Greylock, formed of hard, erosion-resistant rock. Geologists estimate that erosion has since carried some 6 miles of rock off today's mountains.

The Berkshires are part of the uplifted New England peneplain, the old erosional mountain surface that was later lifted and then dissected by water erosion and smoothed by long episodes of glaciation. The hills rise gently on the east from the Connecticut River Valley to a wide plateau atop the range. The western edge of the Berkshires is an abrupt escarpment that drops as much as 1,000 feet to the broad valley that separates the hills from the Taconic Mountains along the New York border.

Because of this mountain barrier, the Berkshire Hills towns and people have historically been isolated, set apart from busy eastern Massachusetts and Boston. The New York Dutch, who settled the lower Hudson Valley by the 1630s, failed to traverse the Taconic Mountains and settle the fertile Berkshire vales. The English, likewise, were unable to penetrate this mountain stronghold from their East Coast colonies, finding the high

Berkshire sunset THINKSTOCK

granite barrier almost impassable. It wasn't until 1725 when Matthew Noble erected a log cabin in today's Sheffield that settlement began. Pioneers eager for new lands came and built houses and villages in the rich river valleys on the west side of the hills.

Towns here prospered during the 19th-century Industrial Revolution, when railroads connected them to burgeoning markets. Industry eventually migrated to the bigger Eastern cities, and farmers migrated farther westward in search of new and better lands, leaving the Berkshire Hills again quiet and unspoiled. These attributes have since attracted visitors who now come to sample the area's pastoral silence as well as its splendid cultural events and festivals. Still, this underpopulated sector of Massachusetts feels ignored by the state government far to the east in Boston. One *Berkshire Week* editorial called for secession from Massachusetts, saying: "Citizens of Berkshire, the time has come to throw off the chains and shackles that bind us to uncaring masters. Let us withdraw from the cesspool of Massachusetts politics and declare that we are the great and sovereign State Of Berkshire."

Stockbridge to Great Barrington

The drive begins at exit 1 on the western end of the Massachusetts Turnpike ("Mass Pike"), I-90. Turn south from the exit onto MA 41. The road runs south through a wide valley shaded with thick woods. A few miles east of here lies the old village of **Stockbridge,** which was settled in 1739 as an Indian mission. Stockbridge, coupled with its sister city Lenox to the north, has long been a bastion of wealth and culture—a Newport in the Berkshires. Some great points of interest in the Stockbridge area include Norman Rockwell's art studio; the Berkshire Playhouse; **Chesterwood,** the home and studio of Lincoln Memorial sculptor Daniel Chester French; and famed **Tanglewood,** the summer home of the Boston Symphony Orchestra since 1937.

MA 41 is a pleasant, narrow road winding through woods west of the meandering Housatonic River. Old stone walls line occasional green pastures, and hills embrace the edges of the broad river valley. To the east looms humpbacked **Monument Mountain,** one of the more famed hills in the southern Berkshires. This craggy peak is not only a superb hiking spot, but also a local literary landmark. On an August afternoon in 1850, writers Herman Melville and Nathaniel Hawthorne were introduced to each other on a hike organized by Oliver Wendell Holmes. The writers and the party's eight other hikers were caught in a torrential thunderstorm just below the mountain's narrow, rocky summit. The party waited the storm out under a granite outcrop, drinking champagne and reciting local poet William Cullen Bryant's tragic poem "The Story of the Indian Girl," an old legend that takes place on the mountain's slopes. The Indian maiden was flung from the summit for loving an enemy warrior. Hawthorne and Melville became fast friends after the incident. Hawthorne returned to Boston not long afterward, while Melville stayed in the Berkshires for 10 more years, writing *Moby-Dick,* his masterpiece novel, which he dedicated to Hawthorne.

To retrace the novelists' ascent, drive north about 6 miles on US 7 from Great Barrington and park. The marked 1.25-mile **Indian Monument Trail** begins here and ends atop the 1,642-foot summit, called Squaw Peak, an hour later. Stunning views of the surrounding Berkshire and Litchfield Hills and the Taconic Mountains unfold beyond the summit.

The first section of the drive ends after 10 miles in **Great Barrington,** the largest town in the southern Berkshires. Incorporated in 1761, the town has long been a haven for poets and philosophers. When attorney William Cullen Bryant, town clerk here in 1816, published his poem "Thanatopsis" at age 23, he was hailed as a literary genius in Europe. His poetic potential never reached beyond those initial accolades, however, and Bryant marched south to New York City and became the influential editor of the *New York Post* newspaper.

View from Monument Mountain
THINKSTOCK

Pumpkin people wait at a bus stop on a back road in the Berkshire Hills.

Great Barrington, an excellent base camp for exploring the area of this drive, is a working, everyday kind of place that is relatively busy for the Berkshires. The town was the first American locale to be lit by electric lights. Inventor William Stanley, founder of the General Electric Company, tested his electrical transformer here by wiring the downtown for streetlights in 1886. The **Albert Schweitzer Center,** a museum and educational facility dedicated to the great doctor, is also located here.

Great Barrington has harbored a large black population ever since slavery was abolished in Massachusetts in 1781. Mum Bet, a servant in Ashley Falls just south of here, filed the 1783 test case that led to her freedom under due process of law and the subsequent abolition of slavery. Fugitive slaves from the south journeyed through the area on the Underground Railroad during the Civil War. Black scholar and pioneering civil rights leader W. E. B. Dubois was born here in 1868.

Other fascinating points of interest are found in the larger Great Barrington region. **Sheffield,** the oldest town in Berkshire

County, has two covered bridges. The **Colonel John Ashley House** is in **Ashley Falls** off US 7 south of town. The restored 1735 house, the oldest in Berkshire County, is a museum that details colonial history and was the site where the Sheffield Declaration was signed in 1773. This document affirmed that all men were created equal and had rights to property.

Nearby is **Bartholomew's Cobble,** a superb 329-acre nature preserve along the Housatonic River near the Connecticut border. The area, with almost 6 miles of trails, offers diverse habitats for plants and animals near two cobbles or cliffs of marble and quartzite along the glassy river. More than 240 bird species have been identified here, along with 740 plant species that include 45 different ferns—more than in any other similar-sized area in the continental United States. The Cobble is a designated National Natural Landmark for its ecologic diversity.

Great Barrington to Woronoco

The next drive segment runs 30 miles east along MA 23 to **Woronoco.** The road follows a section of the old stage route between Boston and Albany, as well as the Knox Trail, a route followed by Colonel Henry Knox during the Revolution. Knox and his men pulled more than 60 tons of weaponry, including 43 cannons and 16 mortars, captured by Ethan Allen at Fort Ticonderoga in 1775. Using ox-drawn sledges, they hauled the arms almost 300 miles in midwinter, giving General George Washington the firepower to enforce the siege of Boston and drive the British out.

Turn east on MA 23 on the north side of Great Barrington. The road initially runs past houses, and after 1.5 miles leaves town and heads up a flat valley flanked by hills. A mile later is the turn to **Ski Butternut,** an intermediate area with a 1,000-foot vertical drop and 8 kilometers of groomed cross-country ski trails. The highway climbs eastward to a forest section uprooted by a violent and rare tornado in 1994. After 4 miles the road crosses the long-distance Appalachian Trail, a footpath that runs from Georgia to Maine. Farther along glistens Lake Buel, half-hidden behind trees.

The turnoff to 10,879-acre **Beartown State Forest** is at 6 miles. This large state parkland encompasses a mostly unspoiled upland region of undulating hills with 1,865-foot Beartown Mountain and 2,155-foot Mount Wilcox the forest high points. Trout streams lace the valleys, while ponds, including 35-acre Benedict Pond, are tucked against wooded ridges. The park offers swimming, fishing, boating, and hiking—5 miles of the Appalachian Trail traverse the park. It also has 12 campsites.

The pretty little village of **Monterey** nestles among hills after 8 miles of the MA 23 drive. The town, settled in 1739 and incorporated in 1847 during the Mexican-American War, was named for the site of an American victory at Monterrey, Mexico. Monterey is strung along the highway, with houses, summer cottages, and a lovely church. A 1927 stone monument honors General Knox and his men for their incredible 1775 winter trek to Boston with Fort Ticonderoga's captured guns. The Bidwell House, listed on the National Register of Historic Places, is a restored 1750 mansion that is open for tours in summer. Past Monterey, Lake Garfield sits just north of a screen of trees. The large lake, named in 1881 for assassinated President James Garfield, offers fishing, boat rentals, and campsites.

The highway continues east, dipping through valleys filled with swamps and beaver ponds and edging over rounded hillsides. The vacation town of **Otis,** sitting at the highway's junction with MA 8, is one of the area's oldest villages. It was named for Harrison Gray Otis, a Massachusetts senator, Speaker of the House of Representatives, and mayor of Boston. The 1828 St. Paul's Church, built in Gothic Revival style, is one of the most picturesque churches in the southern Berkshires. The first nudist colony in the Berkshires was founded near Otis in 1933. Just west of town is Otis State Forest and **Otis Ridge Ski Area,** with 5 lifts and 11 trails.

Continue the drive by zigzagging through Otis on MA 23 then escaping into the hills. The road dips and rolls for the next 10 miles, descending sharply through moist ravines colored with mountain laurel and passing Benton Pond and Otis Reservoir. **Tolland State Forest,** lying south of the highway, is a 4,893-acre area wrapping around 1,065-acre **Otis Reservoir.** The lake offers fishing for bass, bluegill, perch, pickerel, and trout, along with swimming and boating. The forest also has a 94-site campground, with 35 sites along the lakeshore. Past Blair Pond, a small lake on the north named for Hiram Blair, the road scales a long, steep hill to Blandford.

Straddling a high ridge, **Blandford** is a town with a view. As the road descends through town, astounding vistas of the Pioneer Valley spread out to the east. The town was incorporated in 1741 by a group of Scottish immigrants, who dubbed their village Glasgow for their hometown. However, the provincial governor, who had recently arrived from England on the ship *Blandford,* denied their request and named it for the ship. In the early 1800s Blandford became a leading dairy center in western Massachusetts.

Past Blandford the highway runs alongside the Mass Pike, beginning a steep descent down the eastern side of the Berkshire Hills. The road drops into a broad valley, crosses the turnpike, and winds down a steep, curvy road for another mile to its junction with US 20 near Woronoco. Turn left or north onto US 20. The next drive section runs north on US 20 and MA 112 for 21 miles to Worthington Corners.

Into the Berkshire Hills

The highway twists northwest in a broad valley above the west bank of the Westfield River, passing through a spectacular road cut that illustrates the uptilted layers of metamorphic rocks on the eastern edge of the Berkshire Hills. The town of **Russell,** a paper mill town, is a couple of miles up the road. Huntington, settled in 1769, quickly follows. A picnic area sits along the river. Angle right onto MA 112 in town. The road passes some churches and the Huntington Country Store, leaves the village, then bends up a narrow valley alongside the small river. **Charles M. Gardner State Park,** a small 29-acre roadside area shaded by white pines, is 3 miles from Huntington. The park includes a picnic area and a great swimming hole.

The highway passes a junction with MA 66, crosses the river, and threads up into hilly countryside. At 5 miles is a view of Knightville Reservoir and dam. The road crests a ridge and turns through a thick woodland of cedar, pine, and birch along a bouldery creek. Farther along is an unmarked pulloff for **South Worthington Cascade,** a gentle 50-foot waterfall over ledges.

The drive next runs through the Worthingtons—first South Worthington, then Ringville, Worthington Center, and **Worthington Corners,** the largest of the villages. The latter crossroads town is set atop a high plateau, surrounded by houses and hill farms. Another of the region's ubiquitous Congregational Churches is here, adorned with stained glass windows. The highway passes a small pond and a golf course built in 1904 before intersecting MA 143. Turn right onto MA 112/143.

The next 14-mile segment of the drive follows real back roads through a rural landscape in the heart of the Berkshire Hills. The highway heads north through wide fields and heads down a steep hill into a broad valley. Keep north (left) on MA 112 at the highway junction. MA 143 goes east to Chesterfield, a short jaunt that makes a rewarding side-trip. The classic hilltop village of **Chesterfield** holds an 1835 Congregational Church and a small local museum. Like this one, most of the colonial villages in the Berkshires are situated atop hills that, with more sunlight, allowed a longer growing season and were immune from lowland flooding.

Three miles from the highway junction at West Chesterfield is a deep valley carved by the East Branch of the **Westfield River.** Turn right just before the bridge on River Road and drive almost a mile south to **Chesterfield Gorge,** one of the Bay State's lesser-known geologic wonders. Protected in a 166-acre reservation, Chesterfield Gorge is an abrupt 1,000-foot-long chasm incised by the Westfield River into ancient Devonian-age metamorphic bedrock. A trail leads from the parking area along the rim of the 30-foot-deep canyon. In spring the river roars through the narrow aperture, swollen water filling the gorge, while in summer and autumn the river quietly tumbles over worn boulders. Look for long grooves in the cliffs that glaciers etched by dragging boulders encased in ice across the rock surface.

Old hemlocks line the clifftop and cling to the steep walls. Other trees shading the gorge and trail include American beech, white ash, red oak, paper birch, and yellow birch. One yellow birch, the largest of its species in Massachusetts, is at least 14 feet in circumference and 79 feet tall. Ferns fill moist cracks and cover the damp gorge cliffs. The gorge was saved by the Trustees of Reservations in 1929 when some boaters noticed loggers preparing to clear-cut the east side of the gorge. The Trustees stopped the cutting and were able to purchase and preserve the property. Note the stone abutment on the canyon wall from the 1739 High Bridge on the old Boston–Albany Post Road.

Back on the main drive route, head north on MA 112. The next 5 miles follow this classic country lane. Old Colonial homes, tree-lined fields, and a long row of maples lie along the asphalt. The road bends east, drops through a shallow ravine dense with trees, and wends through open pastures with dairy cows. The road joins MA 9 in **Cummington,** a small village that was a flourishing industrial town in the 19th century with textile mills, paper mills, and tanneries. Stop by the restored **Kingman Tavern,** which is also the general store and local post office, for a look back at the past.

To go on, turn right on MA 9/112. The next 7-mile stretch runs east alongside the Swift River in a shallow valley for a few miles before climbing through low hills to the highway's junction with MA 112 North. Turn north (left) on MA 112 and enter

Goshen, a small dairy town with homes, a red barn, and the village cemetery.

A mile out of town is the right turn to 1,770-acre **DAR State Forest.** This parkland is one of western Massachusetts's most popular recreation areas, with visitors filling its 51-site campground, 9 miles of trails, and two lakes every summer weekend. The hilly terrain is studded with rocky tors, including 1,713-foot Moor's Hill and its five-state view from a fire lookout. The forest also has a nature center with programs through the summer.

MA 112 continues north a few miles over hill and dale to its junction with MA 116. Turn west (left) on MA 116. For a side-trip, head north on scenic MA 112 toward the Mohawk Trail, dashing down a broad valley amid low hills. The beautiful village of **Ashfield,** a mile north of this remote highway intersection, is worth a quick visit. The 1812 Town Hall, originally a church, is a stunning edifice topped with a weather-vaned steeple. Many well-kept Colonial homes line the village streets. But unlike most New England villages, Ashfield has no village green.

Over the Hoosac Range

The main drive route heads west on MA 116 for 23 miles over the plateau crest of the **Hoosac Range,** a sub-range of the Berkshire Hills, to Adams. This section of highway crosses a superb landscape, threading across scenic, rolling hills punctuated by occasional distant views broken by picturesque villages and farms. The road runs west for 8 miles to Plainfield, passing fields, farms, and barns. **Spruce Corner,** at 3 miles, holds the small, white clapboard, 1874 Spruce Corner School House. **Plainfield** is another classic hill town, settled relatively late (1770), which flourished with industry in the mid-19th century. It is now an agricultural and tourist center. Stone walls and towering maples line the village streets. The Plainfield Congregational Church, with a gold-domed steeple, dominates the skyline.

The highway rolls west through the wooded hills. The 7,882-acre **Kenneth Dubuque Memorial State Forest** lies north of the drive off MA 8A. This rugged area, part of a mostly wild range that also includes Savoy Mountain and Mohawk Trail State Forests, has 6 miles of hiking trails, 35 miles of mixed-use trails, several ponds, and a thick northern hardwood forest. Stone walls, heaped up by long-ago farmers clearing their rocky fields, edge the tar road. Farther along is a wide valley with a left turn to Windsor State Forest. The forest, 3 miles south, offers 24 campsites, hiking trails, and opportunities for fishing. The small settlement of Savoy, dominated by an old schoolhouse and Baptist Church, is reached after 15 miles.

The highway continues west over this high, upland region to a lofty ridge crest. Here it begins the long descent down the western escarpment of the Hoosac Range to the industrial town of Adams. Mount Greylock, the 3,491-foot high point of Massachusetts, looms to the west. The road drops down steep, wooded vales and past open fields. A few miles later it begins the final abrupt descent into Adams and the broad and fertile Hoosic Valley (also spelled Hoosac).

Adams to Pittsfield

Adams is a good-sized industrial town that spreads along the Hoosic River's banks in the afternoon shadow of towering Mount Greylock. The town was founded in 1766 as East Hoosuck but was later renamed for Samuel Adams, the Revolutionary patriot who led irate citizens to a "tea party" in Boston Harbor in 1773. West Hoosuck is today's Williamstown. The main part of East Hoosuck was later divided into **North Adams** and Adams. The two naturally became rivals, although Adams always asserted it was the original settlement. After the Mohawk Trail highway opened, North Adams erected a sign that read: THIS IS THE CITY OF NORTH ADAMS, THE MOTHER OF THE MOHAWK TRAIL.

Overlooking North Adams, MA Thinkstock

The Adams citizenry, feeling slighted after being ignored in the dedication festivities, put a sign on its north boundary that said: YOU ARE NOW LEAVING ADAMS, THE MOTHER OF NORTH ADAMS AND THE GRANDMOTHER OF THE MOHAWK TRAIL.

Adams grew as a Quaker settlement in the 1700s, and its 1782 Quaker Meeting House is still a local historic landmark. The 19th century brought industrial prosperity to the town. Textile and paper mills, powered by the river, fueled the boom alongside their looming smokestacks. An immense statue of President William McKinley in the town center was erected after his 1901 assassination. Today the town economy relies on industry and a large quarry. Susan B. Anthony, the famed woman suffrage leader, was born here in a simple 2-story frame house.

MA 116 and MA 8 intersect in downtown Adams. To continue the drive, turn south (left) onto MA 8. The road winds through the town's southern outskirts and finally breaks away from the development after 1.5 miles, then runs up the Hoosic Valley. Lofty wooded ridges on Mount Greylock tower to the west. This 3,491-foot mountain, the state's high point, is the focus of the 12,500-acre **Mount Greylock State Reservation.** The peak is a spur of the Taconic Mountains, a long, narrow range that straddles the New York border.

After 5 miles the drive enters **Cheshire.** This village has long been a dairying center. The **Cheese Press Monument,** sitting on the corner of Church and School Streets across from the town post office, testifies to its economic and historic importance. It's also one of the stranger monuments in New England, whose towns usually display Revolutionary or Civil War statues on the village green. The monument, a concrete reproduction of a cheese press, has a sign that says:

Near this spot was made in 1801 the great Cheshire cheese weighing 1235 lbs. one day's product of the town's dairies, moulded in a cider press. It was drawn by oxen to Hudson, N.Y. and shipped to Washington. It was presented at the White House to President Thomas Jefferson as a token of regard from the citizens of Cheshire.

The cheese was well received in the nation's capital, and slices were dispensed to the president, his cabinet, his advisors, and foreign dignitaries. Later the town sent a 100-pound cheese to President Andrew Jackson, who responded with a letter that can be seen in the town's historic **Cole House.** Built in 1804, the Cole House also has an eight-panel door that forms a double cross to protect it from witchcraft.

Cheshire Lake, a long, thin reservoir, is tucked among hills south of Cheshire. The highway runs along its eastern shore, bordered by lots of roadside development and houses. About 12 miles from Adams, the drive meets MA 9. Turn right on MA 9 and enter Pittsfield, the largest town and commercial center in western Massachusetts. A small city with a population of almost 45,000, Pittsfield sits along the upper Housatonic River, which has long provided power for its diverse industries.

Pittsfield, the Berkshire County seat, was settled in 1752 and quickly became a trading and agricultural hub. The town figured in the American Revolution, having declared independence from British authority 3 months prior to the signing of the Declaration of Independence. After the war agriculture could not support the town, so Pittsfield turned toward industrialization and thrived. Mechanized textile mills, using cheap river power, helped fill the nation's demand for clothing during the War of 1812. Paper mills and the establishment of General Electric by William Stanley, who first successfully used alternating current and lit the streets of Great Barrington with electric lights, brought further prosperity.

Today Pittsfield is a busy, working-class town that seems out of place amid the pastoral Berkshire Hills and their small, scattered villages. The town offers travelers not only a wide variety of services, but also some interesting points to visit. The **Berkshire Museum** on Main Street is a superb regional museum

View from Mount Greylock Thinkstock

with 18 galleries that include a collection of Hudson River School landscapes, mobiles by Alexander Calder, and a natural history collection of shells, fossils, an aquarium, and local fauna. Arrowhead is a stately 18th-century house that was home to writer Herman Melville for 13 years in the mid-19th century. It was here in 1850 and 1851 that Melville penned his classic novel *Moby-Dick* about Captain Ahab and his obsession with a great white whale. The spartan house is still furnished with some of Melville's belongings and is open for viewing in summer and fall.

The Berkshire County Historical Society is also located here. East of town off MA 8 is the **Crane Museum of Papermaking,** with displays on papermaking and paper money. The Crane Paper Company is the supplier of paper for US currency.

The drive jogs through Pittsfield. From the junction of MA 8 and MA 9, go west on Dalton Avenue to Tyler Street. Take a left on South Street (US 7), drive through the downtown with its old brick buildings, and in a few blocks go right on US 20. Follow this road, Housatonic Street, through a residential area for just over 4 miles to the intersection of US 20 and MA 41. Go left or south on MA 41.

Hancock Shaker Village

Hancock Shaker Village, one of the most fascinating and popular Berkshire attractions, sits immediately west of this highway junction. To visit it, continue west from the junction on US 20 for 0.5 mile to the village entrance and parking area. The Shaker Community at Hancock, now preserved as a living museum, was the third of 19 Shaker colonies established between 1778 and 1836 in the eastern United States. The village was established in 1790, 14 years after Mother Ann Lee and her disciples came from England as dissident Quakers. The group, calling themselves the United Society of Believers in Christ's Second Appearing, received their later name from their ecstatic worship practices. As they prayed, the spirit moved them with trembling, whirling, dancing,

The round stone barn, built in 1826, is one of the most unusual buildings at Hancock Shaker Village.

and shaking. The Shakers believed Mother Ann to be the female personification of the Messiah after her vision in an English jail when Christ appeared to her and became one with her.

After Mother Ann's death in 1784, the Shakers codified their lifestyle and beliefs in the Millennial Laws, which governed how their utopian communities were run and served as a code of conduct for believers. They dedicated themselves to God; established complete equality of the sexes, although men and women lived apart; held only common property; were pacifists; kept separate from the outside world; and found God and perfection in work. The Shakers were also celibate, which allowed their church to grow only through new believers and adopted orphans.

The Hancock Shaker Community was one of the largest in the United States by the 1850s, with a population of more than 300. The thriving village boasted at least 20 buildings along with fertile gardens, herds of livestock, and prosperous craft

A team of work horses receives well-earned pets from visitors at Hancock Shaker Village.

workshops. The Shakers, with their meticulous craftsmanship and attention to detail, marketed vegetable seeds, invented things such as the clothespin, circular saw, and flat broom, and made simple chairs and ovoid wooden boxes. As the Industrial Revolution gathered steam, however, traditional Shaker markets were flooded with inferior but cheaper goods, turning community reliance to agriculture.

As the Shaker faith emerged into the 20th century, its population of converts slowly ebbed and by the 1950s only a handful remained here. In 1960 the remaining buildings were to be sold by the last Shaker sisters and razed to make room for a racetrack. Local residents raised funds, however, and bought the community and 1,000 acres to preserve the Shaker heritage as an outdoor museum. Today visitors can explore the grounds and brick and wood buildings, delving into the Shaker lifestyle. The

A worn millstone leans against a stone barn at historic Hancock
Shaker Village.

visitor center sells tickets, has a cafe and gift shop, and dispenses information, including a map of the village.

The herb garden, staffed by knowledgeable herbalists, is where the Shakers grew seeds and raised medicinal herbs. The most interesting building and one of the great masterpieces of American folk architecture is the round stone barn built in 1826. Erected in a functional round design, this 3-story dairy barn housed 52 milk cows that one man, standing in the middle, could feed at once. Other buildings of note include the laundry and machine shop; the brick dwelling that housed nearly 100 Brothers and Sisters in separate quarters; the 1795 Brethren's Workshop, where round wooden boxes are still made by carpenter-interpreters; the replica schoolhouse; and the austere 1793 Meetinghouse. Hancock Shaker Village offers a wonderful glimpse back at a little known but intriguing chapter in American religious history. Much of the positive energy and simplicity that the Shakers brought to their unusual community still remains for today's visitors to reflect back on. Remember the old Shaker hymn that begins: "'Tis a gift to be simple, 'Tis a gift to be free."

The last 8 miles of the drive head south from the Shaker Village on MA 41 to West Stockbridge and exit 1 on the Mass Pike. This section runs through open countryside on the east flank of the forest-clad Taconic Mountains. Cornfields, farms, and occasional homes fringe the road. The highway runs through Richmond, now a housing community but once a busy iron ore center. **West Stockbridge** is a small town with an active downtown area that includes restaurants and shops. Its old 1830 **Shaker Mill** on the Williams River is the site of the world's first hydroelectric dam. The drive ends on the south side of West Stockbridge where MA 41 meets exit 1 on I-90.

3 Mohawk Trail Scenic Byway

General description: This 57-mile route follows the Mohawk Trail, one of the nation's first designated drives, through the northern Berkshire Hills between Greenfield and Williamstown and ends by climbing to the summit of Mount Greylock.

Special attractions: Shelburne Falls, Mount Mohawk Ski Area, Catamount State Forest, Deerfield River, Berkshire East Ski Area, Mohawk Trail State Forest, Savoy Mountain State Forest, Florida State Forest, Natural Bridge State Park, Western Gateway Heritage State Park, Mount Greylock State Reservation, Clarksburg State Forest, Williamstown, Sterling and Francine Clark Art Institute, Williams College Museum of Art, scenic views, rafting, kayaking, hiking, camping, fishing.

Location: Northwestern Massachusetts, west of I-91.

Drive route number and name: MA 2, Notch Road.

Travel season: Year-round.

Camping: Public camping is found in several state forests on or just off the drive. Mohawk Trail State Forest has 56 sites; Savoy Mountain State Forest has 45 sites; Mount Greylock State Reservation has 15 tent sites and 7 group sites reached only by trail; Clarksburg State Park has 45 sites.

Services: All services in Greenfield, Shelburne, Shelburne Falls, North Adams, and Williamstown.

Nearby attractions: Deerfield Village, Mount Sugarloaf State Reservation, Hancock Shaker Village, Bennington (VT), Pittsfield State Forest, Berkshire Museum, Stockbridge, Taconic Trail State Park, Beartown State Forest, Bish Bash Falls.

The Route

This 57-mile scenic route follows the Mohawk Trail, the first designated scenic road in New England, from Greenfield in the Connecticut River Valley to the quaint college town of

Mohawk Trail

Williamstown in far northwestern Massachusetts. The drive also makes a 9-mile detour south to the airy summit of Mount Greylock, the state's highest peak. One of New England's most beautiful and famed scenic roads, the Mohawk Trail is a drive to be savored and enjoyed time after time, season after season.

The drive follows a centuries-old footpath blazed by Indians, traverses deep valleys floored by rivers, high wooded ridges and mountains, white farmhouses surrounded by grassy pastures, apple orchards, colonial villages, and a blaze of autumn colors during prime leaf-peeper season. The paved highway is open year-round, although the Mount Greylock spur road closes in winter.

The route also crosses the Berkshire Hills, a southern extension of Vermont's Green Mountains. The Berkshires, comprising a high, rolling plateau without a definite mountain spine, are a remnant of the uplifted New England peneplain. A handful of steep river valleys slice deeply into the range, but nowhere do the rivers cut completely across the formidable Green Mountain–Berkshires upland barrier. This mountain barrier was long an impediment to westward travel, expansion, and settlement. The Mohawk Trail carves a path across an interesting cross-section of the Berkshire uplift. It traverses the Deerfield River Valley before following the deep gorge of the tributary Cold River to the top of the plateau. At the western edge of the plateau, the escarpment drops abruptly 1,000 feet to North Adams and the Hoosic River Valley. Across the wide valley towers Mount Greylock, one of the highest peaks in the Taconic Mountains, a long range that stretches along New York's eastern border from northern Connecticut to central Vermont.

The drive begins on the west side of Greenfield at the rotary intersection of I-91 and MA 2. Go west on MA 2. The actual designated Mohawk Trail begins 20 miles to the east in Orange.

Greenfield & Deerfield

Greenfield, the seat of Franklin County, spreads among green and fertile fields on the west bank of the wide Connecticut River at its confluence with the Deerfield River. The old town, originally settled as part of greater Deerfield in the 1680s, incorporated in 1753 and drew its name from the verdant grasslands blanketing the valley. The town, with a population of about 18,000, has long prospered as an agricultural and industrial center. The country's first cutlery factory opened here in the early 1800s. It retains an interesting Main Street with an eclectic assortment of buildings. A few of these include the Greenfield Public Library and St. James Church, an 1847 reproduction of an English church. The local historical society has a small collection of local artifacts, furniture, photographs, and paintings on display at 3 Church Street.

Before you go much farther, a worthwhile side-trip is **Historic Deerfield** village just south of Greenfield on US 5. **Deerfield,** established in 1663 on the lush river plain, is considered the best-preserved colonial village in New England. Along The Street, Deerfield's main avenue, sit 65 18th- and 19th-century houses and buildings with 13 of them open to the public. For years after its settlement, Deerfield was a remote and dangerous outpost on the edge of the great western wilderness. Two major Indian raids in the years just after its founding decimated the settlement, including the Bloody Brook Massacre on September 18, 1675, when 64 men, most of the village's male population, were killed in an Indian ambush during King Philip's War.

An even worse event occurred one cold February dawn during Queen Anne's War in 1704 when the French led a contingent of 350 Indians into the Deerfield stockade, killing 49 residents, burning much of the village, and capturing 112 prisoners who were promptly marched 300 miles north in the dead of winter to Canada. One eyewitness who survived the attack later recalled, "not long before the break of day, the enemy came in like a flood upon us; our watch being unfaithful." Within 3 years the town was resettled by many of the same families, and flourished through the 1700s as an agricultural center.

Over time neighboring Greenfield usurped Deerfield as the commercial and business center of the upper Pioneer Valley, which kept Deerfield from destroying its old colonial heritage. Now its historic district stands as a charming, elegant reminder of the richness of American life in the 18th century. Almost 6,000 acres of prime farmland surrounding the village have also been acquired and removed from modern development. Historic Deerfield is hard to see in a single day—there is so much to explore. Begin by stopping at the visitor center in Hall Tavern in the heart of Deerfield. Maps, interpretative information, a short film, and admission passes to the buildings are here. Admission to all the dwellings is by guided tour with a costumed interpreter only.

Since it's hard to visit all the interesting sights here, it's best to pick a few and come back another day to visit others. Some of the best buildings include the 1717 **Wells-Thorn House,** once owned by tavern owner Ebenezer Wells; the 1733 **Ashley House** inhabited by Reverend Jonathon Ashley; the 1799 Federal-style **Asa Stebbins House,** a brick home built by a wealthy farmer and decorated with scenic French wallpaper that depicts the South Sea voyages of Captain Cook; and the **Memorial Hall Museum,** which includes a door hacked by Indian hatchets in the terrible 1704 ambush along with a textile museum, silver and metalware collection, and a 19th-century printing office.

Greenfield to Shelburne

The drive begins by heading west on MA 2 from I-91 and Greenfield. The road quickly passes through a business strip mall and bends north into woods and out of town as it arcs around Greenfield Mountain, a high knoll perched above the broad valley. After about a mile is **Shelburne Summit,** with an observation

The Bridge of Flowers, spanning the Deerfield River, brings summer color to Shelburne Falls.

tower that yields a spacious view east across the Connecticut River Valley and north to New Hampshire and Vermont. Continuing westward, the highway swings around the mountain to enter the **Deerfield River Valley** at **Shelburne.** The river lies below the highway in a deep, steep-walled valley. The **Mohawk Trading Post,** the first in a series of "trading posts" along the route that vend American Indian crafts, sits alongside the drive with its prominent totem pole (a Northwest Coast Indian symbol) and teepees (the traveling lodge of the Plains tribes). Farther along are a couple of maple sugar houses, including **Gould's Maple Farm,** which offer sap-to-syrup demonstrations in early spring.

Low hills composed of ancient granites and metamorphic rocks rise beyond the valley and highway. A diverse woodland of white pine, poplar, sugar maple, black locust, American elm, and red oak blankets the hillsides, while willow and sycamore

The frothy Deerfield River crashes over glacial potholes and bedrock, forming spectacular Shelburne Falls.

Glacial potholes in Shelburne Falls, MA
THINKSTOCK

trees shade the riverbanks. After almost 8 miles a spur road, MA 2A, turns south (left) and leads 0.5 mile into the tidy hamlet of **Shelburne Falls.** This 1768 village, named for Salmon Falls and the second Earl of Shelburne, straddles the Deerfield River. It once had a hill-farm economy, but now relies on tourism along with local dairy farms and maple sugaring houses for sustenance. Linus Yale constructed his first Yale locks here in 1851. Its Victorian-style downtown, relatively unchanged since the turn of the last century, is lined with attractive shops, art galleries, and restaurants.

The unusual **Bridge of Flowers** is the main attraction that every Mohawk traveler wants to see at Shelburne Falls. An abandoned 398-foot-long, five-arch trolley bridge, now reserved for pedestrians, is decorated with more than 500 flower species that bloom from spring to fall. The local Shelburne Women's Club cultivates the beautiful and prolific gardens as a war memorial with an ingenious use of the defunct bridge. The bridge actually links Shelburne Falls with the neighboring township of Buckland.

The town's other major attraction is the glacial potholes chiseled into the bedrock by the swirling Deerfield River at a great falls. The symmetrical potholes, ranging from a few inches to more than 40 feet in diameter, formed over thousands of years when the river, laden with melted glacial water and sediments, scoured and polished holes into the metamorphic rock with tumbling cobbles and boulders. The smooth bedrock here is a popular sunning and swimming area on hot summer days.

Back on the drive, the highway reaches its junction with MA 112 just past Shelburne Falls. A left turn on MA 112 leads to the placid 1779 village of **Buckland,** with a classic church, some lovely 1700s houses, and a small museum. A right turn on MA 112 winds up a pretty valley lined with apple orchards and rolling farms to **Colrain.** This small village, basically a church, post office, and town hall with a scattering of homes, is the site of the first school to fly the American flag, an old foundry, and a small covered bridge on Lyonsville Road (one of four 19th-century bridges in Massachusetts). **Catamount State Forest,** a 1,125-acre parkland, lies north of here. This hilly country offers streams, marshes, a 47-acre pond, and 5 miles of hiking trails.

Along the Deerfield River

From here, the drive route heads west up the deepening valley. The **Deerfield River** runs deep and still through this section, its calm waters reflecting trees, sky, and clouds. About 7 miles from Shelburne Falls, the drive reaches **Charlemont,** a snug town along the river's fertile floodplain. This largely rural village was first settled in 1749, when it was known as Chickley's Town and later, Charley Mount. The **Charlemont Historical Society Museum** in the town hall displays local memorabilia. The A. L. Avery & Son General Store has been open since 1861.

White clapboard homes with grassy yards studded with snowball bushes line the highway. Nearby is the rebuilt Bissel Covered Bridge over the Deerfield River. The hills across the valley harbor **Berkshire East Ski Area** and its 1,180-foot vertical drop, 45 trails, and plenty of beginner and intermediate terrain on 400 acres. The Deerfield River in this area offers some of Massachusetts's best trout fishing as well as a challenging 10-mile raft run over Class II and III rapids.

Just past Charlemont, the drive intersects MA 8A, which heads south into the heart of the Berkshire Hills. The road continues west past an old farm amid cornfields and, a mile later, a roadside rest area with picnic tables beside the river. A historical marker here remembers the **Shunpike,** the nation's first toll-free "interstate" road, which followed the river. The site is dedicated to "the thrifty travelers of the Mohawk Trail who forded the Deerfield River here in 1797 rather than pay a toll at the turnpike bridge." This protest helped win the battle for free travel on Massachusetts roads by 1810. Adjacent to the marker is an old cemetery with the remains of many area pioneer families.

The highway crosses the river on the Mohawk Indian Bridge and reaches **Mohawk Park** and its landmark bronze sculpture of a Mohawk with upraised arms on the opposite bank. The statue, placed atop a 9-ton boulder in 1932, honors the five Indian nations that regularly used the **Mohawk Trail.** An arrowhead-shaped tablet at the base reads: HAIL TO THE SUNRISE—IN MEMORY OF THE MOHAWK INDIAN. The valleys that the highway now follows through the northern Berkshire Hills were once traversed by a centuries-old Indian trail leading from the fertile Connecticut Valley to the Mohawk and Hudson River Valleys in New York. This trail was used in 1663 by a warring party of Pocumtuck Indians who invaded Mohawk territory in today's New York. Dutch settlers in Albany forged a fragile peace between the sides, but when Mohawk Chief Saheda was murdered on the trail en route to signing the treaty, the enraged Mohawks retaliated by killing all the Pocumtuck warriors and thus eradicating the tribe.

Later pioneers traversed the Mohawk Trail from the Massachusetts Bay Colony to the Dutch settlements in New York. Their trail grew into a wagon route and then the toll-free Shunpike Road. The Mohawk Trail highway opened on September 1, 1914, and was the first designated scenic auto route in the United States.

Across the Berkshire Plateau

The highway continues west, leaving the Deerfield River and entering a narrow gorge carved by the Cold River through **Mohawk Trail State Forest.** The 6,457-acre forest, straddling river and highway, adjoins 10,500-acre **Savoy Mountain State Forest** to the west, forming the largest slice of undeveloped land in Massachusetts. A mile into the park is a 56-site campground on the north side of the river. Several hiking trails also begin here. The highway follows the narrowing valley, twisting alongside the river as it tumbles and pools over cobbles and boulders.

A dense canopy of trees, including maple, birch, and beech, clots the steep mountain slopes and encloses the asphalt in a green embrace. An abundant understory of azalea, raspberry, wild rose, and mountain laurel blankets the forest floor. Occasional pullouts allow access to the river for trout fishermen and photographers. The Black Brook Road twists south from the canyon and, after a couple of miles, intersects Tannery Road. It then tracks west into Savoy Mountain State Forest and a 0.5-mile, blue-blazed trail that leads to **Tannery Falls.** This beautiful waterfall, tucked into a narrow defile, cascades and drops 80 feet over cliffs and ledges to a placid pool.

After a few miles the highway leaves the Cold River Valley and begins steeply climbing northwest onto the broad, wooded flank of Hoosac Mountain. The road ascends 1,200 feet in the next couple of miles to Whitcomb Summit, the highway's 2,173-foot high point. Here, along with an inn and cottages, is a bronze elk statue and a stone tower that offers far-ranging views. To the north stretch Vermont's Green Mountains. Mount Monadnock, an isolated New Hampshire landmark, sits on the northeast horizon. The rolling Berkshire Hills unfold to the south, and Mount Greylock looms to the west.

The drive, now atop the Berkshire plateau, next runs through **Florida.** This small village, ironically one of the state's coldest places, was founded in 1805 just after the United States purchased Florida from Spain. To reach a great viewpoint north of the drive, go 1 mile past Whitcomb Summit. Turn north (right) on Tilda Hill Road and follow it to a sign that says RAYCROFT LOOKOUT. A one-lane track leads down to a short trail, which in turn leads to a lofty and sweeping viewpoint perched high above the Deerfield River Valley.

Just up the highway is Central Shaft Road, which goes south for 4 miles to Savoy Mountain State Forest. Below the drive route is the **Hoosac Railroad Tunnel,** one of the great engineering feats of the 19th century. The 4.7-mile railroad tunnel, completed in 1873, opened an easy rail route from Boston to Albany and points west by boring through Hoosac Mountain's solid rock base. The epic construction of the tunnel, nicknamed "Bloody Pit," required 24 years of labor, the lives of 196 men, $15 million, and the new explosive nitroglycerin.

Back on the Mohawk Trail, continue to **Western Summit.** Here is the third lookout tower on the route and a marvelous aerial view of Mount Greylock towering above the green valley of the Hoosac River and the patchwork quilt of farms surrounding North Adams. From the overlook the highway bends north and sharply descends from the 1,000-foot-high escarpment on the western edge of the northern Berkshire Hills. Almost 4 miles from Whitcomb Summit, the highway wheels slowly around the famed and scenic Hairpin Turn and a restaurant at its head. The road edges 3 more miles down the Hoosac Mountain wall to North Adams, the bustling commercial hub of northwestern Massachusetts.

North Adams & Mount Greylock

Settled in 1737 and incorporated in 1878**, North Adams** has long been a busy blue-collar town with paper and textile mills along the Hoosic River. The factory town, part of the state's industrial backbone, thrived after the completion of the Hoosac Tunnel, connecting it with Boston and its port. More than 60 percent of Boston's trade came through North Adams and the tunnel by 1895, causing the town to proclaim itself "the western gateway." Most of that industry and its jobs have now passed, and the city relies on a diverse economic base. Fort Massachusetts, a frontier outpost built in 1745, sat just west of today's town and protected the area from marauding Indian attacks—and kept Hudson River Dutch settlers from living in the area. The French and Indians torched the fort in 1746, but it was rebuilt the next year.

The drive enters North Adams, passing old brick mills and warehouses built in the 19th century and the tall spires of churches, including the brick St. Francis of Assisi Church. Beaver

Dense woodlands surround the narrow road to the top of Mount Greylock, Massachusetts's highest point.

Mill, an 1833 mill on Beaver Street, is a historic landmark. The **Western Gateway Heritage State Park,** just south of MA 2 in the old city railroad yard, offers a glimpse into local railroad and industrial history. A large display details the construction and economic impact of the Hoosac Tunnel and includes a replica of a tunnel section complete with dripping water, the sounds of picks against stone, and the deafening explosion and flash of nitroglycerin. Other basic tools used in the tunnel's excavation are seen, including plumb bobs and sighting transits. Amazingly, when the two ends of the almost 5-mile tunnel met mid-mountain, the alignment error was less than 1 inch. The museum is housed in old railroad buildings and surrounded by renovated shops and restaurants.

North Adams also boasts the **Massachusetts Museum of Contemporary Art,** usually called MASS MoCA, in the 19th-century former Sprague Electric Works Factory building. The museum, with art and sculpture galleries and performing arts venues, is considered one of the largest and finest contemporary art museums in the world.

The highway passes the North Adams downtown area and a junction with MA 8. A right turn on MA 8 leads north a short distance to **Natural Bridge State Park,** a 48-acre parkland with a marble natural bridge arching over a narrow, 60-foot-deep chasm. The road twists through the western side of town, passing old houses with steep yards and a sprawling cemetery holding the remains of some of the Hoosac Tunnel fatalities.

Look for Notch Road on the edge of town, which is the turnoff for this drive's summit side-trip. Turn south (left) on the road and drive uphill through houses. The road quickly leaves town and begins a meandering, 9-mile course up the north and west flank of **Mount Greylock,** the 3,491-foot rooftop of the Commonwealth of Massachusetts.

Greylock is a magnificent mountain standing high and aloof over verdant river valleys and towns that skirt its wooded slopes. The isolated peak, separated from the Berkshire Hills by the Hoosac Valley, sits on the eastern edge of the narrow Taconic Mountains. This distinct range runs along the New York border from northern Connecticut to the midsection of Vermont. The centerpiece of the 12,500-acre Mount Greylock State Reservation, the mountain has its own climate because of its height and exposure. Fog and clouds often shroud its windy summit, while heavy rain and snow storms sweep across its wooded slopes.

The road to the top is hemmed in by hardwood forest and climbs steeply. Occasional glades of grass and wildflowers break the woods. After a mile the road enters the park and passes through a beautiful forest of birch floored with ferns. A drive up Mount Greylock is like a telescoped journey to northern Canada's boreal forests. The woodland is initially composed of the northern hardwoods, including yellow and paper birches, and American beech with some hemlock and white pine. Mountain maple, ash, and small shrubs grow higher, above the 3,000-foot level. And finally, near the summit, is the taiga conifer forest of red spruce and balsam fir.

As the narrow lane works its way upward, you may get glimpses of the lower mountains and valleys between tree trunks. The road crosses the white-blazed Appalachian Trail and a day-use parking area for hikers before spiraling up to the mountaintop. A pygmy forest of windswept balsam fir, its branches flagging east away from the prevailing westerly wind, borders the road near the summit. The road emerges at last on the broad summit and a one-way loop. Paved parking areas here allow access to viewpoints, trails, **Bascom Lodge,** and the **War Memorial Tower.** The stone lodge, built in 1937, welcomes overnight visitors and hikers. The 92-foot War Memorial Tower, honoring the state's men killed in wars, pokes high above the summit plateau. A clear day offers a startling view of five surrounding states.

A road continues south from the top, dropping 7 miles to the park visitor center. The reservation comprises more than 35 miles of trails, including an 11-mile segment of the long-distance Appalachian Trail. This drive section is open only from May through October, depending on snowfall and snowmelt.

Williamstown

To continue the main drive, return back down Notch Road to MA 2 in North Adams and turn west (left). The last section of the drive runs 4 miles from North Adams to the colonial village of **Williamstown.** The highway passes through the western outskirts of North Adams, a strip of houses, an old mill, and factory outlets. Outside town the drive rolls across the broad Hoosac Valley and enters Williamstown, the ideal New England college town and home of prestigious Williams College.

Williamstown was established in 1753 by soldiers from nearby Fort Massachusetts, who named it West Hoosuck. Settlers were required to own 5 acres and to build a house that measured at least 15 by 18 feet. Colonel Ephraim Williams, the fort commander and one of the first settlers, wrote a bequest in his will in 1755 to found a free school stipulating that it was in the Massachusetts Bay Colony and the town be renamed for him. Two months later he was ambushed and killed during the French and Indian War, but the terms of his will and the establishment of the college couldn't be carried out until 1791 when a 40-year border dispute between Massachusetts and New York was finally settled. The college and town were then named for their early benefactor. Williams College has since acquired a reputation as one of the nation's finest liberal arts schools with a beautiful campus and a small student body. The college's fine Federal and Georgian-style buildings, many dating from late colonial times, surround the town's village green at the end of the drive.

Williams College is the cultural center of western Massachusetts with 2 excellent art museums. The free **Sterling and Francine Clark Art Institute** is one of the best small museums in the entire United States, with an extraordinary collection that rivals most big-city museums. The institute harbors the nation's largest collection of 19th-century French paintings, including 8 works by Corot, 8 by Monet, and 30 by Renoir. Medieval works include the exquisite *Virgin and Child Enthroned with Four Angels* by Piero della Francesca. The American canvas collection boasts a dozen works by John Singer Sargent as well as work by Frederic Remington, Mary Cassatt, John Kensett, and 10 paintings by renowned Maine artist Winslow Homer. The diverse collection came to Williamstown in the 1950s after the Clarks felt that the town and their art would be safe in the event of nuclear war. Nearby is the Williams College Museum of Art, another free museum, with a permanent collection of some 11,000 pieces.

The Williamstown village green, surrounded by the college buildings, is the end point of this drive. It is a good place to park and roam around town. A nearby tourist office can provide

The First Congregational Church lifts its steeple above the scenic route and the Williams College campus.

maps and brochures. On Main Street is a 1753 house, built to the original zoning specifications for settling in West Hoosuck and constructed with the period tools and materials. The **Williamstown Theatre Festival,** one of New England's great summer theaters, offers more than 200 performances every July and August in the 521-seat Adams Memorial Theater. West of town is **Taconic Trail State Park** and the college's **Hopkins Memorial Forest,** a 2,500-acre nature reserve laced with trails. The Hoosic River offers both canoeing and fishing opportunities. To connect up with the Berkshire Hills Scenic Route to the south, head out of Williamstown on US 7 and follow this scenic road south to Pittsfield.

APPENDIX: SOURCES OF MORE INFORMATION

For more information on lands and events, please contact the following agencies and organizations.

Berkshire Visitors Bureau
3 Hoosac St.
Adams, MA 01220
(413) 743-4500
berkshires.org

Cape Cod Chamber of Commerce
5 Patti Page Way
Centerville, MA 02632
(508) 362-3225,
(888) 33-CAPECOD
capecodchamber.org

Cape Cod National Seashore
99 Marconi Site Rd.
Wellfleet, MA 02667
(508) 771-2144
nps.gov/caco/

Central Massachusetts Convention and Visitors Bureau
91 Prescott St.
Worcester, MA 01605
(508) 755-7400, (866) 755-7439
centralmass.org/

Greater Boston Convention and Visitors Bureau
2 Copley Place, Ste. 105
Boston, MA 02116
(617) 536-4100, (888) SEE-BOSTON (888-733-2678)
bostonusa.com

Massachusetts Office of Travel & Tourism
10 Park Plaza, Ste. 4510
Boston, MA 02116
(617) 973-8500,
(800) 227-MASS
massvacation.com

Mohawk Trail Association
PO Box 1044
North Adams, MA 01247
(413) 743-8127
mohawktrail.com

Mohawk Trail State Forest
175 Mohawk Tr.
Charlemont, MA 01339
(413) 339-5504
mass.gov

Berkshire Chamber of Commerce
75 North St., Ste. 360
Pittsfield, MA 01201
(413) 499-4000
berkshirechamber.com

Provincetown Chamber of Commerce
PO Box 1017
307 Commercial St.
Provincetown, MA 02657
(508) 487-3424
ptownchamber.com

Savoy Mountain State Forest
260 Central Shaft Rd.
Savoy, MA 01247
(413) 663-8469
mass.gov

Shawme-Crowell State Forest
42 Main St./MA Route 130
Sandwich, MA 02563
(508) 888-0351
mass.gov

Tolland State Forest
PO Box 342
410 Tolland Rd.
East Otis, MA 01029
(413) 269-6002
mass.gov

Windsor State Forest
1838 River Rd.
Windsor, MA 01270
(413) 684-0948, (413) 268-7098 (off-season)
mass.gov

INDEX

ABOUT THE AUTHOR

Stewart M. Green, living in Colorado Springs, Colorado, is a freelance writer and photographer for FalconGuides/Globe Pequot and other publications. He's written over thirty travel and climbing books for Globe Pequot, including *Scenic Routes & Byways Colorado, Scenic Driving New Hampshire, Scenic Routes & Byways California's Pacific Coast, KNACK Rock Climbing, Rock Climbing Colorado, Rock Climbing Europe, Rock Climbing Utah, Best Hikes Near Colorado Springs, Rock Climbing New England, Best Climbs Moab, Best Climbs Denver and Boulder,* and *Best Climbs Rocky Mountain National Park.* He's also a professional climbing guide with Front Range Climbing Company in Colorado and is the climbing expert at About.com. Visit him at green1109.wix.com/ stewartmgreenphoto for more about his writing and photography.